Trauma recovery

Nicole Renn

BookLeaf Publishing

India | USA | UK

Presentation by *BookLeaf Publishing*

Web: www.bookleafpub.com

E-mail: info@bookleafpub.com

ISBN: 9789357449083

First edition 2022

DEDICATION

For Mollie. Because every day without you teaches me a hard lesson you protected me from.

ACKNOWLEDGEMENT

There are many people who have made my journey possible but most importantly a close friend Rose Hall for encouraging me to begin my journey and helping through each and every day.
Also my therapist. A necessary in life now.

Therapy

What therapy means to me
Has changed throughout my life.
The choice between a yes or no
Over whether to use that knife.

I've tried to be as normal
As a girl like me can be.
Hid behind my many personas
Not really knowing which ones me.

From that small child that needed protecting
To the adult I am today
I survived those days in between
And I'll always find a way.

My captor will not beat me
My mind is mine to keep
There will be one day in my future
Where it wont disrupt my sleep.

Trauma isn't easy
It's a fight I didn't know I had
Each day my Hope's and dreams
Are dashed with all of the bad.

I'll win the game eventually
And therapy is what I'll thank
I'll be a wholesome human
With so many memories in the bank.

For now the knife is resting
One day it wont exist.
It will be wow just look at her living
Instead of wondering if I'll be missed.

Triggers

My triggers they creep up on me
No matter how hard I try
To know the things that make me bad
And feel like I want to die.

I've won this battle many times
But each time it's like the first
The emotions and feelings that come along
Always feel like they are the worst.

My journey isn't a linear one
It's full of peaks and troughs
I've learnt all this the hardest way
And at the greatest cost.

My triggers they creep up on me
But I'm learning what they are
I'll beat this thing eventually
Whether that time be near or far!

Inner child

I wish that I could tell you
That everything will be fine.
That these feelings that you are feeling
Wont be there all the time.

I wish that I could hug you
And make you see that you
Are worth every tear you're crying
I only wish you knew.

Some people may have failed you
They haven't fulfilled their role
Little do you know but someday
You will be brave and you will be bold.

My inner child was crying
And she needed someones love
She need just some comfort
As she prayed to the lord above.

Dear child I will be the one to save you
I'll comfort you at last
I'll teach you to be happy
And not to live in the past

My inner child is quietly singing
Thanking God that she was safe
That she no longer had to be that strong
Because she's in a better place.

Hope

When everything seems pointless
And you can't see any way
Of overcoming this darkness
Theres some things the future you might say.

There will be things in 6 months time
That make you smile again
You will see light where there was darkness
You may even laugh now and then

The journey isn't easy
And it will feel like an uphill climb
But you have more strength than you know
To see how you can shine.

I know that you feel selfish
And you want to disappear
But I promise it isn't the only way
You can rid yourself of this fear.

There are people around who love you
And need you to stick around
In tiny things there is always hope
No matter how cheesy that sounds.

Be present

I wonder if people see me
In the way I see myself
I wonder if people would hear me
If I said that I needed help

My brain is an over thinker
And I'm always paranoid
That people can't possibly like me
And nothing will fill that void.

I question my every movement
And decision that I make
I hope that one day soon ill be happy
With every step I take

I'm learning to be kind to me
And give myself the time
To look after me and my fears
To own them and make them mine.

It's time for me to be present
In each and every day
Each day I will be happy
In every possible way.

Trust

If I tell you that I love you
I mean it 100%
If it appears that I might trust you
You should know just what that meant

It's so hard for me to believe
That anyone might be
In it for the long haul
And actually care about me

So if I'm missing you and need you
I might want you to be around
Because it's hard for me to trust you
And keep my feet on the ground

Because people always leave me
And let me down all the time
So I need to learn to love you
And put my fears all on the line

I've learnt that you aren't leaving
You are here with me to stay
And I've nearly learnt to trust you
So the days aren't quite as grey

I can see the world in colour
And see that there is hope
For me to be so happy
And find it easier to cope

Strength

Strength is built inside me
And is created by pushing through
I'm constantly being challenged
And proving what I can do

I fight a battle with my will
Whenever I may try
A part of me just wants to stop
Give up and stamp and cry

When i challenge myself i feel stronger
Like I can win any race
And climb each and every mountain
With the biggest smile on my face.

It says up yours to my abuser
It makes me feel that I'm worth
Much more than they ever thought of me
And much more is what i deserve

Expectations

I've been waiting for you to see me
For you to give me what I need
From the day i said please help me
You've not listened as i plead

Now I'm used to being failed by you
And not having my expectations met
And to this little girl that's very sad
That you haven't met my needs just yet.

I'm always full of hope
That one day you might change
That you might suddenly be what I need
I know that might sound strange

I know i need to stop wanting more
And just accept what I have got
You are the person that you are
Even if that hurts me a lot.

I'm grieving that person in my head
And saying goodbye to the what ifs
I'm learning to be that for myself
And ride this mental shift.

Self Care

I sometimes don't feel like trying
Or like everything will be ok
I sometimes just want to sleep
And try again the next day

My brain isn't always upto fighting
If its busy or hasn't had enough sleep
But nothing will be drastically different
And all the problems they will just keep

So I let myself be sleepy
And give myself what I need
Some time to readjust to life
And facilities to get back in the lead

It doesn't mean I'm failing
Or that I'm not good at what I do
It means I'm only human
And i need some down time too

Home isn't home anymore

When I no longer have to see that front door
Or the feeling that I don't belong any more
In that place with stuff all over the floor
Because home is not home any more

Now I no longer have to return
To a place where I never was sure
Where i never felt safe and secure
Because home is not home anymore

I hate that place in my head
Where i continued throughout just to dread
Where things weren't always inside the law
Because home isn't home anymore

Safe place

This is the place I belong
It's my safe place, where I feel strong
Where I feel love and have done all along
Those hard times are behind us, they're gone.

It's a place just for us
You, me and the dogs are a plus
Warmth, safety and honesty are a must
Our safe place is one built on trust.

Our home is our way to escape
From our past and our future will shape
Our new start for us two will be great
We knew it wouldn't be too late

Home is where I'll find you
And you can always find me too
When you are happy or you are blue
We will fight anything, just us two.

Internal voice

My internal voice is bugging me
It's making me believe I'm wrong.
The voice is making me question
All I've known is right all along

It's making me think people hate me
That people don't really care
When in actual fact its teasing me
And all those people are still there

I want to be able to tell the voice
To do one and leave me be
And most of the time I am winning
So I'm more confident within me

Therapy is helping me
And I'm learning to be in control
There are days when the voice still wins
But I'm much better on the whole

Partnership

Just for one day my smile was so big
It was all about being together
Everyone was happy and the place was alight
I don't think I've ever been that happy- not ever

It was a turning point for me and you
We can now be together in solidarity
We told everyone how we felt
And just how happy we planned to be

That day was for us
and showed all that we are
People turned up for us
from both near and far

From that day forward it really felt
Like it was me you and the dogs
Bigger and better than ever
I've found my frog

Trauma medal

Will I suddenly live like normal
And feel like I'm winning at life?
Will I stop feeling sad about history
And start feeling like I've won the fight?

Will it be a great revelation
That I no longer suffer because of you
Will I be confident, brave and together
And living my life like I want to?

Maybe it happens without me noticing
Like I'm an adult and just getting on
And laughing smiling at all the fun things
And the bad times they've all gone

I hope that it happens just like that
And I don't realise it's happened to me
So that I can be thankful for good days
And realise how beautiful life can be.

She was me

I remember her so vividly
So scared to make a change
She hid behind her brick wall
And nothing bad seemed strange

She needed someone to help her
To tell her she could be more
To make her life into something
And finally walk out that door

There was always someone stopping her
And telling her she couldn't be
The person of whom she was dreaming
That person who now is me

I made despite those people
To a place of which I dreamed
A place of no more drama
And happiness now it seems

I am now on control of that person
Who I never thought I could be
I am in charge of my own decisions
And I'll finally live like I'm free

Living in limbo

My brain is in overdrive
It's hard to know what's right
All this stuff whizzing round my head
So it's hard to sleep at night

Just when I think I'm starting to be normal
This thing rears its ugly head
I just want to live like you do
And not worry about going to bed

I'd love to say I'm ok
And that I've recovered from my shit
That I'm no longer living in limbo
And all the pieces fit

One day that will be true for me
I'll succeed and will be free
I'll be living for the here and now
And my priority will be me.

Nightmares

Last night you appeared in my nightmare
You shouted and screamed at me
You told me how I was useless
And I'd never get where I want to

You made me feel like I was nothing
And there was no point being alive
I could see myself at my lowest point
And I'd never get out of that dive.

I should cherish thoughts of you
And think of you with a smile on my face
But instead this is how you manifest
And make me feel all out of place.

I'll shake off the thoughts today
And carry on like I haven't been hurt
I'll go running and forget that you
Hate me and used to treat me like dirt.

My sister

For many years I protected you
And didn't tell you how I felt
I tried to make your life normal
And not understand what I had been dealt

You were young and innocent
And I wanted you to stay that way
I wanted you to grow up happy
And enjoy every single day

Until one day you asked me to tell you
What it was that makes me sad
What it was that made me angry
I why I felt like I was going mad

It took a lot for me to tell you
And change your world forever
It really hurt to throw badness on
The way we grew up together

Once I told you and things were ok
And it felt like I wasn't alone
It's like a new bond had formed between us
Because of the compassion you had shown

My sister you are my hero
And I love you more every day
You took on all my wounds
And told me I'd be ok.

www.ingramcontent.com/pod-product-compliance
Lightning Source LLC
La Vergne TN
LVHW050507210726
843509LV00015BA/3026